TECHNOLOGY, INNOVATION VIS A VIS PATENTS: TRENDS AND POLICY

VOLUME 1, ISSUE 4 OF BRILLOPEDIA

VAISHALI SINGH

Copyright © Vaishali Singh
All Rights Reserved.

ISBN 979-888530969-1

This book has been published with all efforts taken to make the material error-free after the consent of the author. However, the author and the publisher do not assume and hereby disclaim any liability to any party for any loss, damage, or disruption caused by errors or omissions, whether such errors or omissions result from negligence, accident, or any other cause.

While every effort has been made to avoid any mistake or omission, this publication is being sold on the condition and understanding that neither the author nor the publishers or printers would be liable in any manner to any person by reason of any mistake or omission in this publication or for any action taken or omitted to be taken or advice rendered or accepted on the basis of this work. For any defect in printing or binding the publishers will be liable only to replace the defective copy by another copy of this work then available.

Contents

Preface

"Start writing, no matter what. The water does not flow until the faucet is turned on".

-Louis L'Amour

Hundreds of students and professors are contributing their work to Brillopedia, we are here to provide ample information about Law and Contemporary issues. Our aim is to provide a platform for today's generation to express their views and ideas on law and contemporary law.

Author

Vaishali Singh

Publication

This research paper is published in volume 1, issue 4 of Brillopedia

CHAPTER ONE

ABSTRACT

Changes in patenting and licensing behaviour occur against a scenery of changes in industrial innovation processes. Over the last decade, the importance of innovation as a driver of competitive advantage in OECD economies has full-grown. Innovation has become additionally globalised, with little associated medium-sized enterprises (SMEs) taking part in a progressively vital role. These changes have contributed to additional cooperative innovation processes that involve a bigger range of additional various actors and inter-linkages among them. Growing levels of business patenting have helped inventors accept the returns from their investments and expedited co-operation via market-based transactions of data. Patents can play a prominent role in the entire technology life cycle, from initial RD&D to market introduction (demonstration to diffusion), and allow competitive technologies to be protected and licensed to third parties to expand financial opportunities. The disclosure of the invention is an essential consideration in any patent granting procedure. In this way, the patent system is designed to balance the interests of inventors and the public.

CHAPTER TWO

INTRODUCTION

As there are many players involved in facilitating the market success of an innovation, the effective use of the tools of IP will play an important role in reducing risk for the players involved, who may then be able to reap acceptable returns for their participation in the process. IP plays an important role in facilitating the process of taking innovative technology to the marketplace. At the same time, IP plays a major role in enhancing the competitiveness of technology-based enterprises, whether such enterprises are commercializing new or improved products or providing services based on new or improved technology. For most technology-based enterprises, a successful invention results in a more efficient way of doing things or in a new commercially viable product. The improved profitability of the enterprise is the outcome of added value that underpins a bigger stream of revenue or higher productivity. Technological innovation may be classified in several ways: product vs. process, radical (basic or fundamental) vs. incremental (improvement), and disruptive vs. sustaining (sequential and/ or complementary). Other important types of (non-technological) innovations that do not result from scientific and/or technological R&D, but are often crucial for profitably marketing the products and services resulting from the investment made in R&D are marketing innovation, institutional innovation, and complementary innovation.

CHAPTER THREE

CHALLENGES

- Innovation is central to business strategy. Firms in a wide range of industry sectors see innovation and R&D as means of improving their competitive advantage. Between 1990 and 2001 industry-financed R&D in the OECD region rose 51% in real terms from USD 244 billion to USD 368 billion, or from 1.31% to 1.48% of GDP. Much of this growth was driven by high-technology manufacturing and knowledge-intensive service sectors, in particular, ICT and pharmaceuticals – the same sectors that have seen the most rapid increases in patenting (Mairesse and Mohnen, 2003)[1].

- Globalisation of innovation processes. Foreign affiliates of international enterprises accounted for between V-day and Revolutionary Organization 17 November of total business producing R&D within the u. s., France and European nation in 1998, over half-hour within the UK, and sixty-fifth in eire and European country. These investments enlarged by over five hundredths within the OECD space between 1991 and 1998 as corporations set R&D nearer to foreign markets (to adapt the product to native needs) and, progressively, nearer to sources of scientific and technological excellence. The economic process of R&D contributes to international patenting.

- The expansion of ICT and the Internet has accelerated the availability of information on new technologies, making secrecy a less viable strategy. Such codified information can be more easily accessed by competitors who can imitate in a shorter period, thus reducing the efficiency of market-based strategies of appropriation[2].

- New technology-based corporations play a crucial role. within the u. s., R&D in SMEs grew at nearly double the speed of R&D in massive corporations throughout the Nineteen Nineties, with the little corporations increasing the foremost pace. This trend was supported partially by enhanced working capital. Patents are particularly vital to new technology-based companies as a result of such companies typically having few assets apart from their belongings and wish patent protection to draw in working capital. The power to license belongings additional allows their participation within the innovation networks of alternative companies.

- Greater collaboration. The growing technological complexity of merchandise and processes, enhanced technological opportunities created by recent scientific advances (e.g. life sciences, ICT, nanotechnology), fast technological modification, a lot of competition and better prices and risks of innovation square measure forcing corporations to figure in larger collaboration. corporations square measure focusing a bigger share of their R&D on activities that square measure connected to their specific competencies, and square measure getting complementary technologies from alternative corporations, universities and government labs. This trend has been expedited by the growth of ICT, which reduces communication prices. The result has been a fast rise in just about all types of collaboration, from sponsored and cooperative analysis to strategic alliances, mergers and acquisitions, and, notably, technology licensing. Collaboration has been expedited by the growth of markets for technology that give formal, market-based exchanges of data via patent licences. Licensing provides another channel by which proprietary technology is often disseminated and utilized – at a value negotiated by vendee and vendor. Within the OECD/ BIAC survey, hr of responding corporations rumoured enhanced inward and outward licensing over the past decade, and four-hundred thru more enhanced cross-licensing. whereas sensible statistics on inter-firm licensing square measure are lacking, estimates within the uscounsela rise in licensing revenues from USD ten billion in 1990 to quite USD one hundred billion in 2000.

- Technology markets affect economic performance and structure in many ways. They provide a means for the diffusion of patented technologies among a larger number of innovating organisations[3]. In addition, they allow firms to concentrate their R&D resources in areas in which they have relative strength and allow them to rely on others for complementary technologies, possibly improving the overall efficiency of industrial R&D and innovation.

- Technology markets can also provide a channel through which firms sell or license technologies they cannot use themselves, encouraging additional investments in innovation. A growing number of firms report significant revenues from outward licensing of technologies they have developed, but do not intend to commercialise. IBM alone has reported revenues of more than USD 1.5 billion in recent years from technology licences, mostly on a non-exclusive basis. [4]Markets for technology conjointly influence trade and market structures. Technology markets produce niches for brand spanking new varieties of companies, like intermediaries that broker matches between potential consumers and sellers of technology and R&D service companies. The quantity of such companies has adult in recent years, as has R&D performed by technical service companies.

- Technology markets also are necessary to supposed fabless semiconductor corporations that style chips and license them to alternative makers, and to tiny biotechnology corporations that determine drug targets that square measure then accredited to larger pharmaceutical corporations for clinical trials, producing and selling. These corporations lack the complementary assets, like selling and producing, that square measure necessary to with success alter their inventions. However, the total economic effects of markets for technology don't seem to be well understood. It is not clear, for example, how such formalised, market-based transactions complement rather than a substitute for the more informal exchanges of technical knowledge that are recognised as drivers of innovation performance. Nor is it clear how markets for a technology compare with other formalised channels of technology transfer, such as strategic alliances, mergers and acquisitions and collaborative research, in transferring codified and tacit knowledge[5]

[1] TuomasTakalo, Markets for Technology: The Economics of Innovation and Corporate Strategy, by Arora, A., Fosfuri, A. and Gambardella, A. Cambridge and London: MIT Press, 2001.

[2] James E. Bessen& Eric S. Maskin, Sequential Innovation, Patents, And Imitation, SSRN Electronic Journal (2000).

[3] Adam B Jaffe, The U.S. patent system in transition: policy innovation and the innovation process, 29 Research Policy 531-557 (2000).

[4] Competition and Regulation Issues in the Pharmaceutical Industry, 4 OECD Journal: Competition Law and Policy 102-222 (2002).

[5] OECD (2003), Turning Science into Business: Patenting and Licensing at Public Research Organisations, OECD, Paris.

CHAPTER FOUR

REVISITING THE WORKING OF PATENT SYSTEM

An immediate issue is to assess how new areas of technology and knowledge are addressed by the patent system. Software, genetics, and business methods are the most recent and are soon to be followed by proteins and nanotechnology[1]. New areas are subject to controversy: should they be patent subject matter at all? How to ensure that patent protection in these areas is not mainly an instrument for rent-seeking and blocking access? How to equip patent offices with the ability to grant patents of sufficient quality in these new areas (e.g. relevant breadth, sufficient inventive step, etc.)?

As the patenting tradition evolves based on experience gained in established fields, accommodating new fields is not straightforward. Patent offices faced this problem previously when chemicals and pharmaceuticals became the patent subject matter. The issue is twofold: i) to analyze the economic impact of patent protection in these fields and compare it with alternatives, such as copyright or no specific legal protection at all; and ii) to have patent offices rapidly accumulate experience in new fields to avoid early-stage mistakes. Databases of prior art should be set up rapidly[2].

In addition, criteria for granting or rejecting applications and for giving patents an appropriate breadth should be clarified as rapidly as possible after the patentability of the subject matter has been decided (more rapidly than was the case for biotechnology and software).

A second issue is the quality of patents. Low-quality patents are people who defend inventions of restricted novelty or that offer to a fault broad protection. Quality patents may be expensive to society. Their proliferation not solely swells the number of patents and patent applications that has to be reviewed by potential innovators and patent offices, however additionally creates uncertainty concerning the validity and social control of patents. The social edges of such patents square measure probably to below, they will, however, be leveraged by their holders for rent-seeking purposes: they will be used as a threat against alternative firms, particularly little ones, or as a part of patent thickets for closing market access to potential competitors.

The more important patents become to innovation and economic performance, the more necessary it is to improve the quality of granted patents and to do so at a reasonable cost. Various means have been already set in place in different jurisdictions and could be considered by others:

- An opposition system looksAssociate in Nursing Economical Manner of guaranteeing the standard of patents: once a granted patent is revealed, third parties will oppose the choice at the agency, wherever an indoor court examines the case as well as any new proof provided within the opposition method. The positive European expertise supports this approach, which ought to be rigorously examined by alternative offices.

- A centralised court system is necessary for ensuring higher legal certainty of enforcement and the validity of rights. The United States pioneered this with the creation of the CAFC in 1982, Japan is following step now with an IP high court, and it is key to the success of the future Community patent that Europe does the same[3].

- International co-operation for promoting quality at the lowest cost. Current negotiations at WIPO (Substantive Patent Law Treaty, SPLT) and formal cooperation among the trilateral offices go in this direction[4].

[1] OECD (2003, Genetic Inventions, IPRs and Licensing Practices: Evidence and Policies, OECD, Paris.

[2] Samuel Kortum& Josh Lerner, Stronger protection or technological revolution: what is behind the recent surge in patenting?, 48 Carnegie-Rochester Conference Series on Public Policy 247-304 (1998).

[3] Walsh, J.P., A. Arora and W.M. Cohen (2003), Effects of Research Tool Patents and Licensing on Biomedical Innovation in Patents in the Knowledge-based Economy, the National Academies Press, Washington, DC

[4] Levin, R.C., A.K. Klevorick, R.R. Nelson and S.G. Winter), Appropriating the Returns from Industrial R&D, Brookings Papers on Economic Activity783-820(1987)

CHAPTER FIVE

CONCLUSION

The enlargement of technology markets may be a major accomplishment of a well-functioning legal system, as these markets enhance the circulation of technology. Our information on technology markets remains inadequate, and future studies ought to be dedicated to it and addressing several of the queries that haven't been, however totally investigated: however do they work? However, will data flow between the varied actors? However, are agreements settled? What's the role of intermediaries?

What is the impact of technology markets on technology diffusion and competition? To what extent, and during which areas if any, do market transactions on technology substitute for the non-market event. As technology markets act with necessary government issues - notably competition - there's a requirement for additional reflection on the economic impact of sure instruments like cross-licensing and patent pools. Additionally, governments are a unit, probably necessary actors in technology markets as they sponsor most simple analysis that's then commissioned by PRO's. Government policies on patenting and licensing practices at execs affect certain segments of the market, like users of basic science. Additionally loosely, one may wonder if these markets are a unit confronted with sure failures which may justify some quite government intervention, particularly as regards SMEs. On this basis, policies may well be designed to support the event of markets for technology and take away barriers that may hamper their development.

www.ingramcontent.com/pod-product-compliance
Lightning Source LLC
Chambersburg PA
CBHW072147150726
48002CB00004B/1674